A GUIDE TO READING
SHAKESPEARE'S *MACBETH*

A GUIDE TO READING

SHAKESPEARE'S *MACBETH*

MARIA FRANZISKA FAHEY

Maria Franziska Fahey is the author of *Metaphor and Shakespearean Drama: Unchaste Signification*, which was shortlisted for the 2012 Shakespeare's Globe Book Award. She is a member of the faculty at Friends Seminary, where she has taught English for more than twenty years.

First Printing, 2012
Second Printing, 2013, contains a new preface, reorganized appendices, and minor revisions of the text.
Third Printing, 2014, contains corrections and minor revisions of the text.
Fourth Printing, 2020, contains minor revisions of the text.
Fifth Printing, 2021, contains minor corrections.

ISBN-13: 978-0-615-73195-7
ISBN-10: 0-615-73195-3

Accabonac Press
61 Jane Street, Suite 17C, New York, NY 10014

Cover illustration and design by Lauren Simkin Berke

CONTENTS

PREFACE

On the Pleasures & Challenges of Reading Shakespeare's Dramatic Language

Reading Shakespeare's plays can be immensely pleasurable, but doing so is no easy task. Whereas we now get a great deal of our information through visual images, including photographs and film, in Shakespeare's day most information came through spoken language. Part of the fun, and also the challenge, of reading a Shakespeare play is having to transform language into visual images for ourselves.

Indeed, Shakespeare was aware of the demands he was making of his audiences. In the Prologue to his play *The Life of Henry the Fifth*, the Chorus admits it cannot bring King Henry himself or "the vasty fields of France" into the theater and so asks the members of the audience to let the play work on their "imaginary forces" (*Henry V* Pro. 12, 18). The Chorus goes on to suggest, "Think, when we talk of horses, that you see them, / Printing their proud hoofs i'th' receiving earth" (Pro. 26-7).

A Shakespeare play is largely "talk"—a series of conversations among a cast of characters. However, the talk of a Shakespeare play is often more difficult to understand than ordinary speech because it has been crafted to bring a whole world before our eyes. The series of questions in this guide is designed to help you listen carefully, scene-by-scene, to what the characters say so that you can use your "imaginary forces" to see the world of *Macbeth* for yourself. As you read the play's language and begin to envision its world, it will be helpful to remain aware of how the language spoken by characters in the play is different from that of ordinary speech. Here are a few of these differences:

Vocabulary. Written over 400 years ago, the plays are known for their unusually large vocabularies, including many words that were, at the time, new to the English language—some probably invented by Shakespeare himself. Almost all readers find the rich vocabulary of a Shakespeare play challenging to understand even as they come to enjoy the subtle and abundant connotations of the words Shakespeare chose. Furthermore, twenty-first century readers will find that the meanings of some words have changed since Shakespeare's day and that other words, rarely spoken now, have become obsolete. For instance, the word *behind* in Macbeth's remark that "The greatest is behind" (*Macbeth* 1.3.117) can mean *still to come*. Be sure to consult the notes in your copy of the play and to keep a good dictionary at hand, one that provides older meanings of words. (Check your library's print or online version of *The Oxford English Dictionary*—the *OED*—which is the most comprehensive English dictionary.)

But don't feel obligated to look up every word when first reading a play. You can understand a great deal about unfamiliar words from their context. For instance, after Macbeth wonders if all the water in the sea could wash the blood from his hand, he decides:

> No, this my hand will rather
> The multitudinous seas incarnadine,
> Making the green one red.   (*Macbeth* 2.2.59-61)

You might not know what *incarnadine* means. But you can figure out that if Macbeth thinks his bloody hand will make a green sea turn red, then *incarnadine* must mean *to make red*. (The *Oxford English Dictionary* indicates that "incarnadine" means "To dye or tinge with incarnadine; to redden.")

~ Poetic Language. The conversations in a Shakespeare play are no ordinary conversations: they were crafted by a poet-playwright who used sound, rhythm, and imagery to convey his meanings. Consider Macbeth's remark near the end of the scene in which he sees a dagger leading him to murder:

> Whiles I threat, he lives:
> Words to the heat of deeds too cold breath gives. (*Macbeth* 2.1.59-60)

In ordinary speech, someone would likely say, "Words *give too cold breath* to the heat of deeds." But Shakespeare's word order allows the lines to rhyme—"lives" with "gives"—which adds a sense of determination to Macbeth's decision to go ahead with the murder. These lines also invite us to imagine how words could stop action with the image of the breath (of speech) cooling down something hot. Sometimes Shakespeare's language demands a bit of extra thinking as we listen for the meanings of a character's words along with the meanings added by sound, rhythm, and imagery.

~ Descriptions that Provide Context. Although Shakespeare's theater included costumes and some props, it did not include sets or lighting. (The use of electricity was centuries away, and plays were performed at The Globe, an open-air theater, in the mid-afternoon.) Audiences would have to glean important context from the characters' speeches. For instance, in act 3, scene 3 of *Macbeth*, we learn that it almost is nighttime when a character poetically describes the last light of dusk and remarks that any traveller out so late would be hurrying to secure a place in an inn:

> The west yet glimmers with some streaks of day.
> Now spurs the lated traveller apace
> To gain the timely inn [.]   (*Macbeth* 3.3.5-7)

Nowadays the time of day and setting could be shown to a theater audience with lighting design and a painted set. Thus, contemporary playwrights usually don't write such descriptions into characters' speeches, and contemporary audiences don't have to decipher and picture them.

~ Implied Action. Unlike stories or novels, most plays don't have a narrator who tells us what characters are doing as they speak to each other. Playwrights can indicate specific actions with stage directions, but Shakespeare's plays have relatively few. Instead, the dialogue itself gives clues about characters' actions. Consider, for instance, what King Duncan says as he praises Banquo:

> Noble Banquo,
> That hast no less deserved, nor must be known
> No less to have done so, let me enfold thee
> And hold thee to my heart.   (*Macbeth* 1.4.29-32)

King Duncan's lines let us see that he extends his arms toward Banquo and hugs him: the king asks to "enfold" Banquo and "hold" him to his "heart." Imagining the world of a Shakespeare play depends, in part, on listening for clues to characters' actions. (Try staging a scene with some friends: doing so will help you become attentive to such clues.)

Learning to see the world of a Shakespeare play by reading or hearing its language takes some work and some patience. However, paying close attention to the play's language will give you access to the most interesting, complicated, and surprising aspects of the plays. As the Prologue to *The Life of Henry the Fifth* shows, Shakespeare invited and relied on his audiences to envision the worlds of his plays, and Shakespeare gave us incomparable language from which to do so. There are always many ways to imagine a phrase, line, or scene, but it's important to start with accurate observations of the play's language.

Using This Guide

The series of questions for each scene will help you to observe the sometimes complex and dense language accurately and to puzzle through the characters' conversations. Before trying to answer the questions for a particular scene, read through the entire scene aloud. Or, better yet, gather some friends, take parts, and read the scene aloud together. Don't be shy: you might mispronounce a word or need to read some lines slowly, but you will have a much better chance of understanding the lines when you read them aloud—and you likely will have more fun. Then, read through the scene again slowly, answering the questions as you go. If you don't fully understand a question, quote the phrase or line that you suspect contains the clues for its answer. Once you reach the scene's end, return to those questions to see if you have been able to figure out anything further.

Some of the questions use terms and refer to methods with which you may not be familiar: they may ask you to observe and analyze "meter" or "figurative language," especially "metaphor." Don't worry if you are not familiar with these terms or if you never have "scanned a line of verse" or "sorted a metaphor's tenor and vehicle": you will find the necessary background information and sample analyses in the appendices. Appendix 1, "Listening for Meter," explains how to identify the basic rhythms of Shakespeare's poetry; appendix 2, "Reading Figurative Language," explains how to identify and analyze figures of speech; and appendix 3, "On How an Edition of *Macbeth* Is Made," explains how the copy of *Macbeth* you are reading is derived from the earliest text of the play and lets you know what kinds of additions and changes an editor may have made in preparing the play for publication. You may find it helpful to read through these appendices before you begin to answer the questions. Or you may consult them when you arrive at a question that requires your knowledge of the information they provide. All of the information in the appendices aims to help you to understand and envision the play for yourself.

Quotations in this guide are taken from the edition of *Macbeth* edited by Burton Raffel and published by Yale University Press in 2005. Following standard scholarly practice, quotations are followed by a citation that indicates the act, scene, and lines from which a passage is quoted. So, for instance, "(3.1.6-7)" refers to act 3, scene 1, lines 6-7. If you are reading a different edition of the play, your line numbers may be slightly different. *(For an explanation of how the differences in editions come about, see appendix 3, "On How an Edition of* Macbeth *Is Made," on page 93.)*

Hearing & Seeing Performances

If, after trying to read aloud by yourself and with friends, you continue to have trouble getting the gist of what the characters are saying to each other, try to locate a good audio recording of the play, one that has been recorded by a cast of experienced Shakespearean actors. (Many libraries have them available.) Read along as you listen to the audio recording of the scene you are working on. Hearing trained actors deliver the characters' lines will likely help you understand much of what the characters are saying. Keep in mind that the way an actor speaks a line depends on that actor's interpretation of it and that you might have another interpretation.

After reading the play, you might enjoy seeing a performance of it. Check to see if there is a live performance at a nearby theater, or borrow a film of the play from your library. If you wait to see a performance until after reading the play, you will be able to compare the way you have imagined the play-world to the way a particular director has. If you see the performance before you've read the play, be aware, as you read, that the particular director's vision of the play is not the only possibility: one good way to do so is to see two, or more, performances or films.

There are many books and websites that publish summaries and analyses of Shakespeare's plays. Be wary. Don't accept another reader's vision of the play too easily: your own careful reading and imagining might lead you to a far more interesting one!

.

QUESTIONS TO CONSIDER AS YOU READ *MACBETH*

Larger Questions

As you answer the questions for each scene, you often will be prompted to think about the topics listed below. If you are particularly interested in one of these topics, you might find it helpful to keep track of what various characters say about it by marking relevant passages in your text or by keeping a list of relevant passages in a notebook. When you have finished reading the play, you then will be ready to consider the collection of passages you have gathered and ask yourself what the play as a whole might be suggesting about the topic. This kind of work is one way to prepare to write an essay about *Macbeth*.

1. **Loyalists, Rebels, & Traitors**. Who rebels? Who is loyal? What do various characters say about rebellion? About traitors? When do characters criticize rebellion? When do they praise it?

2. **Men, Women, Children, & Beasts**. What do various characters say about what it means to act like a man? A woman? A child? A beast? Do any of the characters in the play conform to any of these stated ideals? Do they defy others?

3. **Political Titles.** What do various characters say about political titles, including those of king and thane? How do characters gain political titles? How do they lose them?

4. **Violence**. What do various characters say about violence, including killing? When do characters consider violence legitimate? When do they consider it wrong? When brave? When cowardly?

5. **Time**. How do various characters speak about time? What do they observe about natural cycles and progressions of time, including day and night, the seasons, and the past, present, and future?

6. **Imagination & Reason.** What do characters assert about imagination? About reason? About the relationship between the two?

7. **Desire, Thought, & Deeds**. What do characters assert about the relationship between thinking and doing? Between desiring and doing?

8. **Visions & Dreams**. To what do characters attribute visions and dreams? How do characters understand them? What is their effect on waking life?

9. **Sights, Pictures, & Appearances**. What do characters assert about how pictures and appearances relate to things themselves? What do they say about things looking like or resembling other things? What do characters say about the effects of seeing?

10. **Fate & Prophecy**. How do characters understand fate? To what extent do characters think prophecy can foretell fate reliably or accurately?

11. **Witches, Weird Sisters, & Wayward Sisters**. Who are the Witches? What powers do they have? What powers do other characters in the play think they have? Who calls them "weird sisters" or "wayward sisters"? What else are they called?

> In Shakespeare's day *weïrd* was also spelled *weyard* and meant "having the power to control the fate or destiny of human beings" (*OED* 1). *Wayward* meant "disposed to go counter to the wishes or advice of others, or to what is reasonable" (*OED* 1a). In the earliest surviving text of *Macbeth*, which is in the First Folio, the Witches are three times called "weyward sisters," once "weyard women," and twice "weyard sisters." Some modern editors print *weird* for the Folio's "weyward" and "weyard"; others print *wayward* for the Folio's "weyward." *(See appendix 3, "On How an Edition of* Macbeth *is Made," for an introduction to the First Folio.)*

12. **Equivocation**. Who equivocates? For what purposes? Who is accused of equivocation?

> Equivocation expresses something technically true that is not the whole truth. Equivocation can, thus, mislead a listener to believe something untrue. But equivocation also can lead a receptive listener to understand a speaker's belief that has been expressed only partially. Because equivocation simultaneously masks and suggests what a speaker knows or believes, it can protect a speaker who expresses a dangerous view from being held accountable for his or her beliefs.

Patterns of Figurative Language

Questions for each scene also will prompt you to notice and analyze figurative language. *(See appendix 2 on pages 86-92 for an introduction to figurative language.)* Sometimes one instance of figurative language echoes figurative language from other scenes in the play. These patterns of figurative language are an important part of how the play is structured and delivers its meanings. You might find it helpful to keep track of repeating figures by marking instances of them in your text or by keeping a list in a notebook. When you have finished reading the play, you then will be ready to ask yourself what the pattern suggests or means. In *Macbeth*, be on the lookout for figures of:

1. **Gardens & Farms**: planting, harvest, trees, fruit

2. **Clothing**: robes, vestments, dress

3. **Theater**: player, prologue, acts

4. **Alcohol and Other Spirits**: drunkenness, wine, supernatural spirits

5. **Sickness & Health**: infection, disease, medicine, physic

ACT 1, SCENE 1

1. Read the scene aloud, with friends if possible.

    a. What do you notice about the meter of the Witches' speech? Scan a few lines of it. *(See appendix 1 on pages 83-5 for an introduction to meter and scansion.)*

    b. What do you notice about its rhyme scheme?

    c. What do the meter and rhyme scheme make the speech sound like?

2. What special abilities do the Witches seem to have? First jot down two lines or phrases that provide important clues and then explain what each clue indicates about their abilities.

3. What might the Witches mean when they say, "Fair is foul, and foul is fair" (1.1.10)? Give two, or more, possibilities. (As you ponder the line, you might want to consider how it would it be different if the Witches were to say, "Fair *seems* foul, and foul *seems* fair.")

ACT 1, SCENE 2

1. What does Malcolm tell his father, the King, about the Sergeant (1.2.3-5)?

2. What does the Sergeant report (1.2.7-23)? Against whom is Macbeth fighting on behalf of the King?

3. Look carefully at the simile describing Macdonwald and Macbeth: "Doubtful it stood, / As two spent swimmers, that do cling together and choke their art" (1.2.7-9).

    a. To what does "it" refer in "Doubtful it stood"?

    b. Analyze the simile by figuring out the tenor for each part of the vehicle. I have done the first one for you. *(For an explanation of these terms and method, see pages 86-91 of appendix 2, "Reading Figurative Language.)*

vehicle	:	tenor
two spent swimmers	:	two battle-weary soldiers
cling together	:	
choke their art	:	

    c. What does the vehicle of the drowning swimmers suggest about the nature of the battle?

4. What is the Sergeant's attitude toward being a "rebel"? Quote a relevant phrase in your answer.

5. How exactly does Macbeth kill Macdonwald (1.2.16-23)? What does Macbeth do with Macdonwald's head?

6. Upon hearing the Sergeant's report, how does Duncan refer to Macbeth (1.2.24)? Quote the line:

7. EXTRA OPPORTUNITY. Consider the Sergeant's tricky simile. (Note that "whence" means *from where* and "'gins" is short for *begins*.)

   As whence the sun 'gins his reflection
   Shipwrecking storms and direful thunders break,
   So from that spring whence comfort seemed to come,
   Discomfort swells. (1.2.25-8)

   a. Continue reading through 1.2.33 and then answer: what event in the battle is the Sergeant describing with the simile above?

   b. The simile compares "the sun 'gins his reflection" to "that spring whence comfort seemed to come." To what in the battle do both compare?

   c. The simile compares "Shipwrecking storms" to the spring from which "Discomfort swells." To what in the battle do both compare?

   d. What does the vehicle of suddenly changing weather suggest about the nature of the battle?

8. To whom does the Sergeant compare sparrows and eagles? To whom does he compare the hare and the lion?

    a. Analyze the similes:

       <u>vehicle</u>   :   <u>tenor</u>

       sparrows   :

       eagles   :

       hare   :

       lion   :

    b. What do these vehicles of animal predators and their prey indicate about Macbeth and Banquo in battle?

    c. EXTRA OPPORTUNITY. For "As sparrows eagles" (1.2.35), editor Burton Raffel notes, "as sparrows eagles=as sparrows dismay eagles (i.e. not at all)" (7). Although Raffel asserts that Macbeth and Banquo are the eagles, some readers might argue that they are the sparrows and that, therefore, they were quite dismayed. What makes the Sergeant's simile ambiguous? How does the line make sense to you? *(For an explanation of an editor's role in printing a Shakespeare play, see appendix 3, "On How an Edition of* Macbeth *is Made," on page 93.)*

9. Count the number of similes and metaphors the Sergeant uses in his three speeches. How many are there? How does hearing all of this figurative language make you feel as you read (or hear) the scene?

10. Summarize what we learn from Ross:

    a. about Norway:

    b. about the Thane of Cawdor:

c. about Macbeth:

d. about the outcome of the "broil":

11. When Duncan orders the Thane of Cawdor to be killed, he says, "Go pronounce his present death" (1.2.64). What does the language of Duncan's order show about the word of the king? (How would it be different, for instance, if he had said, "Go execute Cawdor"?)

12. With what title does Duncan tell Ross to "greet" Macbeth (1.2.65)?

13. "What he hath lost, noble Macbeth hath won" (1.2.67). What earlier line in the play does Duncan's statement echo? Quote it.

14. By the end of this scene, what has been revealed about how a king is defended?

15. Very little has been revealed about why the rebellion is taking place. What is the effect of not knowing? How does this scene make you feel about the rebellion and the rebels?

ACT 1, SCENE 3

1. What do the Witches call each other (1.3.1, 1.3.3)?

2. Note the opening of the Witches' chorus: "The weyward sisters, hand in hand" (1.3.33). Some editors understand "weyward" as *weird*; others understand it as *wayward*. *(See "Larger Questions" page 2 for explanations of* weird *and* wayward.*)* What weird things do the Witches claim to be doing? Quote one. What wayward things do they claim to be doing? Quote one.

3. Notice Macbeth's first line in the play (1.3.39).

    a. Write it down:

    b. What might Macbeth mean? Give two possibilities.

    c. Whose earlier line in the play does Macbeth's line echo?

4. Using Banquo's description (1.3.40-8), draw a picture of the Witches.

5. With what three titles do the Witches address Macbeth? List them.

6. What is Banquo trying to find out when he asks the Witches, "Are ye fantastical, or that indeed / Which outwardly ye show" (1.3.54-5)?

7. Banquo then asks:

   If you can look into the seeds of time
   And say which grain will grow and which will not,
   Speak, then, to me[.] (1.3.59-61)

   a. Analyze the metaphor:

   <u>vehicle</u>   :   <u>tenor</u>

   seeds/grain   :   _____

   _____   :   time

   grow   :   _____

   not grow   :   _____

   b. What does the idea that time has seeds, and that some will grow and some will not, suggest about the future?

   c. What does the idea suggest about Banquo's attitude toward the Witches' abilities to see the future?

8. What do the Witches tell Banquo?

9. To what does Banquo compare the origins of the Witches (1.3.80-1)?

10. "Would they had stayed" (1.3.83). Why does Macbeth wish the Witches had stayed? Quote and cite a statement of Macbeth's that provides a clue.

11. Banquo wonders if "such things" were "here as we do speak about" (1.3.84) or if they have "eaten on the insane root / That takes the reason prisoner" (1.3.85-6). What would happen to someone if the insane root took their reason prisoner? Try drawing a picture of a person with this condition. Be sure to show what is going on inside his or her head.

12. How does Banquo react when Ross, directed by the king, calls Macbeth "Thane of Cawdor" (1.3.107)? How does Banquo refer to the Witches?

13. Analyze Macbeth's metaphoric response to Ross's news: "Why do you dress me / In borrowed robes" (1.3.108-9).

    a. <u>vehicle</u> : <u>tenor</u>

       dress me :

       borrowed robes :

    b. Think about the qualities of robes. What does the vehicle *robes* suggest about the nature of political titles and positions?

14. "Glamis and Thane of Cawdor! / The greatest is behind" (1.3.116-17). Note that in Shakespeare's day, "behind" could mean "in the past" (*OED* 1c), but it also could mean "still to come" (*OED* 4). (The future was often represented as "behind" because a person cannot see the future.) What might Macbeth mean when he says "the greatest is behind" if:

    a. behind means "still to come"?

    b. behind means "in the past"?

c. EXTRA OPPORTUNITY. If you were performing the role of Macbeth, which meaning you would choose for *behind*? Explain why.

d. What does Macbeth's comment show about his attitude toward the Witches?

15. Reread Banquo's comment:

And oftentimes, to win us to our harm,
The instruments of darkness tell us truths,
Win us with honest trifles, to betray's
In deepest consequence. (1.3.123-6)

a. How does Banquo refer to the Witches now? Quote the phrase.

b. What would be the "honest trifles"?

c. Explain Banquo's phrase "to win us to our harm."

d. EXTRA OPPORTUNITY. If you were performing Banquo, with what tone would you say these lines? Underline the words you would stress.

e. EXTRA OPPORTUNITY. If you were performing Macbeth, how would you react to Banquo's speech? Write a stage direction for Macbeth.

16. Carefully reread Macbeth's speech from 1.3.127-42 ("Two truths are told . . . But what is not"). The speech is difficult to follow because of its many questions and cryptic statements.

   a. "Two truths are told, / As happy prologues to the swelling act / Of the imperial theme" (1.3.126-8). To what "two truths" does Macbeth refer?

   b. From what world are the vehicles of Macbeth's metaphoric language fetched? (Prologues? act? theme?)

   c. What does Macbeth's figure of the two truths as "prologues" imply about the third of the Witches' greetings, namely, "king hereafter"?

   d. Macbeth says, "This supernatural soliciting / Cannot be ill, cannot be good" (1.3.130-1). What questions does he then ask in support of this assertion? Paraphrase them.

   e. What might be "the horrid image that doth unfix [Macbeth's] hair / And make [his] seated heart knock at [his] ribs, / Against the use of nature" (1.3.135-7)?

   f. Where is this horrid image?

   g. If for Macbeth "nothing is / But what is not" (1.3.141-2), what is Macbeth's reality like? (In this context "but" means *except*.) Describe it.

h. Macbeth realizes that "chance may crown [him], / Without [his] stir" (1.3.143-4). How would Macbeth be crowned *with* his stir? What title or titles has Macbeth received without his stir?

i. What does Macbeth's soliloquy reveal that Macbeth is thinking about Ross's news that he is the Thane of Cawdor?

j. What does Macbeth's soliloquy suggest about his attitude toward what he is imagining?

17. Banquo explains Macbeth's "rapt" state to Angus and Ross by explaining that "New honors come upon [Macbeth], / Like our strange garments, cleave not to their mould / But with the aid of use" (1.3.144-6). Analyze the simile:

<u>vehicle</u>	:	<u>tenor</u>
strange garments	:	
cleave not	:	
their mould	:	
aid of use	:	

What does Banquo's metaphor imply about political honors and titles?

18. EXTRA OPPORTUNITY. "Kind gentlemen, your pains / Are registered where every day I turn / The leaf to read them" (1.3.150-2). To what does Macbeth's metaphor compare the act of remembering? What does he imply his mind is like? Try making an illustration of his metaphor.

ACT 1, SCENE 4

1. Malcolm describes that Cawdor "died / As one that had been studied in his death / To throw away the dearest things he owed, /As 'twere a careless trifle" (1.4.8-11). What does Malcolm's simile describing Cawdor's execution suggest about Cawdor's demeanor at the time of his death?

2. What does Duncan mean when he says, "There is no art / To find the mind's construction in the face" (1.4.11-12)? (In this context "art" means *skill*.) Before deciding what Duncan means, be sure to consider his next sentence, "He was a gentleman on whom I built / An absolute trust" (1.4.13-14).

3. Why does Duncan tell Macbeth, "More is thy due than more than all can pay" (1.4.21)? For what does Duncan feel in debt to Macbeth?

4. How does Macbeth, in his response to Duncan, characterize the relationship between king and subject (1.4.22-7)?

5. When Duncan says that he has "begun to plant" Macbeth and "will labor / To make [him] full of growing" (1.4.28-29), to what does he compare himself? Sort the metaphor's vehicle and tenor.

<u>vehicle</u>   :   <u>tenor</u>

6. How does Banquo extend Duncan's planting metaphor? Quote the lines.

7. Who is the Prince of Cumberland? What is Macbeth's concern about him (1.4.48-50)?

8. Reread Macbeth's aside: "Stars, hide your fires, / Let not light see my black and deep desires, / The eye wink at the hand. Yet let that be / Which the eye fears, when it is done, to see" (1.3.50-3).

   a. Why does Macbeth want the stars to hide their fires?

   b. Why does he want the eye to "wink" (to close its lid) and not see what the hand is doing?

   c. What does Macbeth mean when he says, "Yet let that be / Which the eye fears, when it is done, to see"? What does he want to see done that his eye fears to see being done?

   d. What do you notice about the rhyme and meter of Macbeth's speech here (1.4.48-54)? Effect?

9. What is ironic about Duncan's saying to Banquo about Macbeth, "He is full so valiant" (1.4.54)?

ACT 1, SCENE 5

1. As the scene opens Lady Macbeth is reading a letter from her husband.

   a. Macbeth has written about the Witches, "I have learned, by the perfectest report, they have more in them than mortal knowledge" (1.5.2-3). To what knowledge does Macbeth refer as more than "mortal knowledge"?

   b. Look back at what Macbeth says immediately after the Witches address him and Banquo. Fill in the blanks:

      "Stay, you _____ speakers, _____" (1.3.____).

   c. Why might Macbeth now think their report is "the perfectest"? (Note that perfect means *complete* as well as *flawless*.)

   d. What does Macbeth call the Witches (1.5.7)?

   e. How does Macbeth address his wife (1.5.10)? Quote the phrase.

   f. To what does Macbeth refer as the "greatness . . . promised" Lady Macbeth?

   g. What does Macbeth's letter show about his relationship to his wife? Quote two (or more) specific phrases and derive your answer from them.

2. Lady Macbeth asserts that Macbeth "shal[l] be / What [he is] promised," but what does she fear about his "nature" and why (1.5.13-16)?

3. What does Lady Macbeth intend to do when her husband arrives?

4. What is the "golden round" (1.5.26)?

5. Lady Macbeth calls on the "spirits" to "unsex" her (1.5.39).

   a. If Lady Macbeth is unsexed, what will she no longer be?

   b. List what she presumes will happen to her when she is unsexed.

   c. What does this list show that Lady Macbeth believes comes with being female?

6. With what three titles does Lady Macbeth greet her husband? What earlier greeting does her greeting echo?

7. Note: "Thy letters have transported me beyond / This ignorant present, and I feel now / The future in the instant" (1.5.54-6). Of what is the present ignorant?

8. What does Lady Macbeth mean when she tells Macbeth, "Your face, my Thane, is as a book where men / May read strange matters" (1.5.60-1)?

   a. Analyze the simile by listing all the parts of the vehicle and tenor and then figuring out the correspondences.

   <u>vehicle</u>   :   <u>tenor</u>

   b. What does Lady Macbeth's simile imply about what people who see Macbeth's face will know?

9. What does Lady Macbeth mean when she instructs her husband to "Look like the time" (1.5.62)?

10. What other instruction does Lady Macbeth give her husband? Quote the simile and metaphor she uses (1.5.63-4).

11. If you were playing Lady Macbeth, what might you do as you say, "Leave all the rest to me" (1.5.71)?

12. If you were playing Macbeth, how might you react to this remark? Give two possibilities.

ACT 1, SCENE 6

1. As the scene opens, where are Duncan and Banquo? About what are they speaking?

2. How does Lady Macbeth treat Duncan? How does she speak to him?

3. EXTRA OPPORTUNITY. Make a quick sketch of Duncan's simile that Macbeth's "great love, sharp as his spur, hath holp him / To his home before us" (1.6.23-4). (A spur is "a device for pricking the side of a horse in order to urge it forward, consisting of a small spike or spiked wheel attached to the rider's heel" (*OED* 1).)

ACT 1, SCENE 7

1. Reread Macbeth's soliloquy at 1.7.1-28 ("If it were done . . . And fall on the other").

   a. "If it were done when 'tis done, then 'twere well / It were done quickly" (1.7.1-2). How many times does Macbeth use the word "it" in this first sentence? (Don't forget that 't=it.)

   b. In the second sentence Macbeth names "th' assassination" (1.7.2). What might Macbeth's delay in naming "it" suggest?

   c. Read aloud: "If th' assassination / Could trammel up the consequence, and catch / With his surcease success" (1.2.2-4). What is the most prominent sound in these lines? What does it make Macbeth sound like?

   d. "If it were done when 'tis done, then 'twere well / It were done quickly." What might Macbeth fear could not be "done" even if the assassination were "done"? In other words, to what does Macbeth refer with the first "it" of this sentence? (Review the speech that follows as you to try to figure out what he means.)

   e. What would be the "be-all and the end-all—here" (1.7.5)? Where is "here"?

   f. What is Macbeth willing to "jump" for the "be-all and the end-all—here" (1.7.6)?

g. Why is Macbeth considering that "We still have judgment here" (1.7.18)? What does he worry "even-handed justice" could make happen to the "ingredients of our poisoned chalice" (1.7.10-11)?

h. How, according to Macbeth, is Duncan "here in double trust" (1.7.12)? (The first reason has two parts.)

i. Macbeth lists yet another reason not to "bear the knife" against Duncan (1.7.16). What is it?

j. What does Macbeth imagine will happen upon Duncan's murder—his "taking off" (1.7.20)? What will Duncan's virtues do? What will pity be like? Notice all the personification.

k. What does Macbeth say is the only "spur" he has to "prick the sides of [his] intent" (1.7.25-6)?

l. Lady Macbeth's entrance interrupts Macbeth's speech. If it hadn't, what might Macbeth have concluded? Finish his line and write one more. Try to write in iambic pentameter.

And falls on the other _____

_____

2. When Lady Macbeth comes to find out why Macbeth has "left the chamber" (1.7.29), Macbeth announces that they "will proceed no further in this business" (1.7.31).

   a. To what "business" does Macbeth refer?

   b. What reasons does Macbeth give Lady Macbeth for not proceeding?

   c. How do these reasons compare to the reasons he articulates in his soliloquy?

   d. Why might Macbeth give Lady Macbeth the particular reasons he does?

3. Of what does Lady Macbeth accuse her husband of being "afeard" (1.7.39-40)? What, according to Lady Macbeth, would make him a "coward" (1.7.43)?

4. Macbeth says that he dares do "all that may become a man" (1.7.46)—that he dares to do what is suitable for a man to do. He adds, "Who dares do more is none" (1.7.47)—that is, who dares do more is not a man.

    a.   What "more" could Macbeth do that would make him "none," that is, not a man?

    b.   What, with this assertion, does Macbeth suggest is an essential quality of being a man?

    c.   What does Lady Macbeth think Macbeth has implied he would be if he dared to murder Duncan (1.7.47)?

5. Lady Macbeth counters, "When you durst do it, then you were a man, / And, to be more than what you were, you would / Be so much more the man" (1.7.49-51).

    a.   What does Lady Macbeth suggest is an essential quality of being a man?

    b.   What does Lady Macbeth say would make Macbeth "so much more the man" than only daring to kill Duncan?

6. How does Lady Macbeth illustrate her point about the importance of keeping one's word? What does she claim she would do if she had sworn to do so?

7. Briefly summarize Lady Macbeth's plan for the murder.

8. A "warder" is a "soldier or other person set to guard an entrance" (*OED* 1).   In what way is "memory" the "warder of the brain" (1.7.65)?

9. What reason does Macbeth give for telling Lady Macbeth to "Bring forth men-children only" (1.7.72)?

10. How does Macbeth intend to "mock the time" (1.7.81)?

11. EXTRA OPPORTUNITY. Define each of Macbeth's two uses of the word *false*: "False face must hide what the false heart doth know" (1.7.82).

    false face=

    false heart=

ACT 2, SCENE 1

1. Describing the night, Banquo comments, "There's husbandry in Heaven: / Their candles are all out" (2.1.4-5)? (*Husbandry* is the management of a household.)

    a. What is the tenor of the vehicle "candles"?

    b. If you were making a film of *Macbeth*, what other clues in the text would help you decide how you would film the opening of this scene (2.1.1-11)? List two clues and say what each suggests.

2. Why does Banquo not want to sleep? For what help does he ask the "Merciful powers" (2.1.7)?

3. When Banquo tells Macbeth he "dreamt last night of the weird sisters," Macbeth responds, "I think not of them" (2.1.18-20).

    a. What does Banquo's dream add to our understanding of why he is reluctant to sleep? What specifically might Banquo have dreamed about?

    b. EXTRA OPPORTUNITY. Argue either that Macbeth is lying or telling the truth when he claims not to think of the weird sisters. (Ground your argument in a specific reference to the text.)

4. When Banquo agrees to Macbeth's proposal that Banquo shall gain "honor" if he "cleave[s] to [Macbeth's] consent" (2.1.23-4), Banquo names a condition: "So I lose none / In seeking to augment it, but still keep / My bosom franchised and allegiance clear, / I shall be counseled" (2.1.25-8).

    a. Allegiance to whom? Explain Banquo's condition in your own words.

    b. What does Banquo's response show that he imagines Macbeth might speak to him about? How might Banquo fear he could lose honor?

5. Reread Macbeth's speech at 2.1.32-63 ("Is this a dagger . . . or to hell).

    a. What does Macbeth try to determine when he asks the dagger that he can see but not clutch, "Art thou not, fatal vision, sensible / To feeling as to sight? Or art thou but / A dagger of the mind, a false creation, / Proceeding from the heat oppressed brain" (2.1.35-8)? In other words, what would the dagger be, and whose creation, if it were a "dagger of the mind, a false creation"? What would it be, and whose creation, if a "fatal vision"?

    b. "Thou marshall'st me the way that I was going" (2.1.41). Who or what is "thou"? How can Macbeth be marshaled the way that he was going?

c. What does Macbeth conclude about the "gouts of blood" he sees on the dagger's blade and dudgeon (2.1.45)?

d. Macbeth personifies "murder" as "Alarumed by his sentinel the wolf" (2.1.51-2). If you were playing Macbeth, what would make sense to do as you say, "thus with his stealthy pace . . . Moves like a ghost" (2.1.53-5)?

e. EXTRA OPPORTUNITY. Shakespeare's poem *The Rape of Lucrece* retells the Roman legend of how Tarquin rapes Lucrece, who then kills herself. If Macbeth moves toward Duncan "With Tarquin's ravishing strides" (2.1.54), then:

vehicle		tenor
Tarquin	:	_____
_____	:	Duncan
_____	:	the murder

What does this metaphor imply about Duncan? About murdering him?

f. EXTRA OPPORTUNITY. If you were choosing music for this scene, what would you choose to convey its mood?

ACT 2, SCENE 2

1. As you read the opening of this scene (2.2.1-16), figure out about what sound effects you would need to stage it. Indicate theses sounds by adding them as stage directions to your text or by jotting them down here with citations.

2. As the scene opens, what does Lady Macbeth describe having done?

3. What, according to Lady Macbeth, stops her from killing the king herself? Quote the phrase.

4. Reread 2.2.13-20 ("My husband? . . . to say a sorry sight") aloud with a friend. What do you observe about Macbeth and Lady Macbeth's speech? What does it tell you about their state of mind?

5. Lady Macbeth tells her husband, "These deeds must not be thought / After these ways. So, it will make us mad" (2.2.31-2). ("Mad" means *insane* in this context.) What does Lady Macbeth mean? After what "ways"?

6. Why might Macbeth hear a voice that says he "murder[ed] sleep" (2.2.34)? Give two possibilities.

31

7. With what metaphors does Macbeth describe sleep (2.2.34-8)? List them:

8. Given what Macbeth says about sleep, if he has murdered it, what will life be like now?

9. Reread the questions Lady Macbeth asks and the instructions she gives her husband, starting with "Go get some water" (2.2.44-8).

    a. What has Macbeth brought with him back to their chamber?

    b. What had been the plan?

    c. What does Lady Macbeth instruct her husband to do?

10. Lady Macbeth says, "the sleeping and the dead / Are but as pictures" (2.2.51-2). ("But" means *only* in this context.)

  a. How are the sleeping and the dead "as pictures"?

  b. What does Lady Macbeth imply about how pictures should affect Macbeth?

  c. How did the sleeping Duncan's appearance affect Lady Macbeth?

11. With what will Lady Macbeth "gild" the faces of the grooms? How will "it seem their guilt" (2.2.54-55)? How does the pun on gild/guilt work? (A *pun* is the use of a word in a statement that simultaneously suggests two or more meanings of the word and, thus, two or more ways to understand the statement. A speaker can make a pun on a word that has more than one meaning or on a word that sounds like another word.)

12. What, according to Macbeth, will "all great Neptune's ocean" not be able to do (2.2.58)?

13. What, in contrast, does Lady Macbeth say about water (2.2.65)? Quote her line and memorize it.

14. What does Macbeth mean when he says, "To know my deed, 'twere best not know myself" (2.2.71)?

15. In his last line of the scene, for what does Macbeth wish?

ACT 2, SCENE 3

1. A *porter* is "a gatekeeper, esp. at the entrance of a fortifed town or castle" (*OED* 1). Where does this Porter imagine he is working?

2. What does the Porter imply about people when he says that a "porter of Hell gate...should have old turning the key" (2.1.1-2)?

3. When had the Porter gone to sleep? What had he been doing? (2.3.23-34)?

4. Notice that the Porter speaks in prose, not verse. How does this affect our sense of his character? (*See appendix 1, pages 83-4 for an explanation of* prose *and* verse.)

5. How does the Porter explain his assertion that drink "provokes and unprovokes" lechery (2.3.26-33)? Quote the line.

6. How does the Porter's joke about drunken desire for sex echo what Lady Macbeth has said about her husband's drunken desire to be king? Look back at 1.7.35-41 and quote the most important lines for this comparison.

7. *Macduff*   I know this is a joyful trouble to you,
            But yet 'tis one.
   Macbeth   The labour we delight in physics pain. (2.3.45-7)

   What meaning does Macbeth's statement convey to the play's audience that Macduff could not understand?

8. Lennox describes the night that has just passed (2.3.52-9). What sound effects would you need for a soundtrack of this night? List them.

9. When Macbeth and Lennox ask him why he is so alarmed, Macduff replies:

> Most sacrilegious murder hath broke ope
> The Lord's anointed temple, and stole thence
> The life o' the building. (2.3.66-8)

   a. Sketch the metaphor with which Macduff describes the murder:

   b. Chart the metaphor's vehicle and tenor.

      <u>vehicle</u>   :   <u>tenor</u>

10. EXTRA OPPORTUNITY. Notice that Macduff won't answer Lennox's question about "his Majesty" directly: "Do not bid me speak. / See and then speak yourselves" (2.3.71-2). Why might Macduff not want to speak about what he has seen?

11. How is "downy sleep, death's counterfeit" (2.3.75)?

12. What had Lady Macbeth said earlier about the "sleeping and the dead" (2.2.51)?

13. EXTRA OPPORTUNITY. "The wine of life is drawn, and the mere lees / Is left this vault to brag of" (2.3.94-5). Analyze this metaphor:

<u>vehicle</u>	:	<u>tenor</u>
wine	:	
is drawn	:	
mere lees	:	
vault	:	

14. Notice that when Macbeth says he has killed Duncan's guards, Macduff asks Macbeth, "Wherefore did you so?" (2.3.106). ("Wherefore" means *why*.)

    a.   With what tone might Macduff ask this question? What does the question suggest that Macduff might be wondering?

    b.   What explanation does Macbeth give for having killed the king's attendants (2.3.107-17)?

    c.   Was killing the guards part of Lady Macbeth and Macbeth's plan?

    d.   What does Macbeth call "reason" (2.3.110)? Fill in the blank: "the _____, reason."

    e.   How does Macbeth describe the king's body (2.3.110-12)?

15. What has Macbeth been talking about when Lady Macbeth faints?

16. What is the consequence of her fainting? What conversation stops?

17. Some directors and critics imagine that Lady Macbeth only pretends to faint. Give a reason that she would pretend to faint.

18. Then give a reason that Lady Macbeth would faint for real.

19. What reasons do Malcolm and Donalbain give for their plan to flee Scotland? Where will Malcolm go? Where will Donalbain go?

ACT 2, SCENE 4

1. When the Old Man remarks on the "sore night" (2.4.3), what does Ross say about the heavens to explain why the night was so strange (2.4.5-6)?

2. How does Ross describe the day (6)?

3. What "unnatural" occurrences do the Old Man and Ross describe (2.4.10-19)? List two.

4. To what does the Old Man link these "unnatural" events (2.4.11)?

5. How does Macduff respond to Ross's asking whether it is "known who did this more than bloody deed" (2.4.22)? Quote the line.

6. Why has Macbeth gone to Scone?

7. Macduff tells Ross he is not going to Scone. What does Macduff's decision suggest?

8. "God's benison go with you, and with those / That would make good of bad, and friends of foes" (2.4.40-1).

    a. How do you understand the Old Man's benison (blessing)?

    b. What earlier lines does the benison echo?

ACT 3, SCENE 1

1. What does Banquo suspect about how Macbeth got what "the weird women promised" (3.1.2-3)?

2. What is Banquo remembering when he wonders if truth will come from the weird women's saying that he will he be the "root and father / Of many kings" (3.1.5-6)?

3. How would Banquo be "set up in hope" by the weird women's oracles (3.1.9-10)?

4. At what event does Macbeth request Banquo's presence?

5. Where is Banquo going during the day?

6. Macbeth tells Banquo, "We hear our bloody cousins are bestowed / In England and in Ireland, not confessing / Their cruel parricide, filling their hearers / With strange invention" (3.1.29-32).

   a. Who are "our bloody cousins"?

   b. Of what does Macbeth accuse them?

   c. What might motivate Macbeth to say this to Banquo now?

43

7. Carefully reread Macbeth's speech at 3.1.49-73 ("To be thus is nothing . . . And champion me to th' utterance").

   a. "To be thus is nothing, / But to be safely thus" (3.1.49). To what does Macbeth refer with the word "thus"? How would he be "safely thus"? Fill in the blanks with words that explain what Macbeth is likely saying:

   To be _____ is nothing, / But to be _____.

   b. What reasons does Macbeth give for his fears of Banquo?

   c. What part of the Witches' prophecy about Banquo does Macbeth remember? What does Macbeth call the Witches here?

   d. Macbeth asserts that "Upon my head they placed a fruitless crown, / And put a barren scepter in my grip, / Thence to be wrenched with an unlineal hand, / No son of mine succeeding" (3.1.62-5). What figurative language does Macbeth use? About what does he complain?

   e. What does Macbeth suspect he has done for "Banquo's issue" (3.1.66)? ("Issue" here means *offspring* or *child*.)

f. Explain what Macbeth means when he says that he has given his "eternal jewel . . . to the common enemy of man" (3.1.69-70). What is his eternal jewel? Who is the common enemy of man?

g. "Rather than so, come fate, into the list, / And champion me to th'utterance" (3.1.72-3). (A *list* is "a space in which tilting matches or tournaments were held" (*OED* 9a).) Rather than accept the prophecy about Banquo's issue, Macbeth challenges fate into the list for a fight. In doing so, what does Macbeth reveal about his attitude toward fate? Toward the Witches' prophecy?

h. What does this speech reveal about Macbeth's values? About his conscience? Indicate the phrases from which you derive your answer.

i. What does the speech reveal about Macbeth's desire to be king?

8. For what does Macbeth tell the murderers Banquo is to blame (3.1.76-87)?

9. What do we learn about the social condition of these men who are willing to murder for Macbeth?

10. Reread Macbeth's exchange with the Murderer at 3.1.89-94 ("Do you find . . . We are men, my liege").

    a. If a man lived according to the gospel, what famous teaching of Jesus would he follow?

    b. What does Macbeth mean when he asks the men if they are "so gospeled" (3.1.91) to pray for Banquo despite all Banquo has done to harm them?

    c. When the First Murderer answers, "We are men, my liege" (3.1.94), what does he imply? How might he fill in the blank: "We are men, not _____." (Hint: what kind of men would follow the gospel most closely?)

11. a. For what reason does Macbeth list all the different types of hounds? What comparison does he eventually make between hounds and men?

    b. Through his comparison of hounds and men, what is Macbeth saying indirectly to the murderers? How would this idea persuade them to kill Banquo?

12. a. Why, ultimately, do the murderers say they will do the killing (3.1.111-17)?

    b. What do their reasons show about the social condition of some men in Scotland?

13. a. What reason does Macbeth give for not "sweep[ing] Banquo from his sight" (3.1.123) even though as king he has the right to do so?

    b. What does Macbeth's reasoning imply about a king's power?

14. Why would Macbeth want to be sure that Fleance is killed?

15. Why might Macbeth order the murder of Fleance only at the very end of his conversation with the Murderers?

ACT 3, SCENE 2

1. Reread what Lady Macbeth says when alone. ("Nought" means *nothing*.)

    > Nought's had, all's spent,
    > Where our desire is got without content.
    > 'Tis safer to be that which we destroy
    > Than by destruction dwell in doubtful joy. (3.2.4-7)

    a. Explain how desire can be "got without content."

    b. To what does Lady Macbeth likely refer as "that which we destroy"?

    c. What does Lady Macbeth think would be "safer" than to "dwell" (live) in "doubtful joy"?

    d. What does this soliloquy show about how Lady Macbeth is feeling?

2. Reread Lady Macbeth's speech at 3.2.8-12 ("How now . . . What's done is done").

    a. Write a stage direction for Macbeth that would account for Lady Macbeth's remarks. How would Macbeth look or what would he do?

    b. What advice does Lady Macbeth give her husband?

c. If you were playing Lady Macbeth, with what tone would you speak when alone? With what tone would you speak to your husband?

3. Analyze Macbeth's metaphor, "We have scorched the snake, not killed it. / She'll close and be herself, whilst our poor malice / Remains in danger from her former tooth" (3.2.13-15). Chart its vehicle and tenor:

<u>vehicle</u>   :   <u>tenor</u>

4. What reason does Macbeth give that it is better to "be with the dead" (3.2.19)?

5. Compare what Macbeth says here to Lady Macbeth's soliloquy at 3.2.4-7 ("Nought's had . . . ").

6. How does Lady Macbeth respond to her husband's worries? Does she share her own?

7. "O, full of scorpions is my mind, dear wife!" (3.2.36)

    a.   What are scorpions?

    b.   If Macbeth's mind is full of scorpions, what must be the state of his mind?

8. Of what knowledge does Macbeth want Lady Macbeth to "be innocent" (3.2.45)? Considering their earlier collaboration, what might motivate Macbeth to keep this information from her?

9. Why would Macbeth want the "seeling night" (3.2.46) to come?

10. Why might Lady Macbeth "marvel" at Macbeth's words?

11. Explain Macbeth's assertion, "Things bad begun make strong themselves by ill" (3.2.55). (Note that "ill" can mean *evil* or *wickedness*.)

ACT 3, SCENE 3

1. What is the effect of a third murderer appearing after the scene in which Macbeth makes arrangements with only two? What does the appearance of the third murderer suggest about Macbeth?

2. Before he dies, Banquo encourages Fleance to escape. What does he say that Fleance may do (3.3.17)?

ACT 3, SCENE 4

1. As the scene opens, how is Macbeth performing his duties as king? Is he meeting his previously stated goal of "mak[ing] our faces vizards to our hearts" (3.2.34)? (A *vizard* is a mask.)

2. How would you characterize Macbeth's conversation with the Murderer during the feast? How would you stage this conversation?

3. What makes Macbeth's "fit" come again (3.4.22)?

4. With what metaphor does Macbeth describe Banquo and Fleance (3.4.31-3)? Quote and analyze it.

5. Reread Lady Macbeth's statement to her husband:

    >   To feed were best at home.
    > From thence, the sauce to meat is ceremony.
    > Meeting were bare without it. (3.4.37-9)

    a. Analyze the metaphor:

    <u>vehicle</u>   :   <u>tenor</u>

    sauce   :

    meat   :

    b. Lady Macbeth's metaphor also contains a pun. On what word does she pun? To what effect? *(See question 11 on page 33 for an explanation of* pun.*)*

6. What causes Macbeth's "fit" (3.4.57)?

7. If you were a Lord or Lady at the banquet, what would you think was happening if you heard Macbeth say to something visible only to him, "Thou canst not say I did it. Never shake / Thy gory locks at me" (3.4.53-4)? (Remember that you could not yet know that Banquo has been killed, but you would know of another recent murder.)

8. How does Lady Macbeth explain her husband's "fit" to their guests (3.4.55-60)?   What would motivate her to say, "My lord is often thus, / And hath from his youth" (3.4.55-6)?

9. "This is the very painting of your fear" (3.4.63).

   a. To what does "this" refer?

   b. What does Lady Macbeth emphasize about such "paintings"?

10. What does Macbeth say "is more strange / Than such a murder is" (3.4.85-6)?

11. How does the banquet end?

12. Reread 3.4.60-111 and notice the seven references to *man, woman, grandam,* and *girl.* Pay careful attention to the context of the remarks and note what each implies it means to be male, to be female, to be young, or to be old. I have done the first one as an example.

a. Lady Macbeth: "Are you a man?" (3.4.60)

> After Lady Macbeth urges the lords not to regard Macbeth's fit, she asks her husband this question. She implies that a man would not be overcome by his imagination and disrupt a feast by talking to a ghost.

b. Lady Macbeth: "these flaws and starts . . .would well become / A woman's story at a winter's fire, / Authorized by her grandam." (3.4.65-8)

c. Lady Macbeth: "What, quite unmanned in folly?" (3.4.76)

d. Macbeth: "What man dare, I dare." (3.4.102)

e. Macbeth: "Or be alive again . . . If trembling I inhabit then, protest me / The baby of a girl." (3.4.106-9)

f. Macbeth: "Why, so. Being gone, / I am a man again." (3.4.110-11)

13. How would Macbeth benefit from keeping "a servant fee'd" in the house of Macduff and the other lords (3.4.135)?

14. What reasons does Macbeth give for planning a visit to the "weird sisters" (3.4.136)?

15. Reread:

> I am in blood
> Stepped in so far that, should I wade no more,
> Returning were as tedious as go o'er.
> Strange things I have in head, that will to hand,
> Which must be acted ere they may be scanned. (3.4.139-43)

   a. Make a quick sketch of Macbeth's image of being "in blood / Stepped in so far" that "Returning were as tedious as go o'er."

   b. What does Macbeth imply about the choice of continuing to murder?

   c. Why does Macbeth feel he must "act" the "strange things" that are in his head?

   d. What does this statement show about Macbeth's mind?

16. "Season" can indicate a time of year or a flavor for food. Using each meaning, give two different explanations of Lady Macbeth's metaphor for sleep, "the season of all natures" (3.4.144).

ACT 3, SCENE 5

1. Who is Hecat? How do the Witches seem to be related to Hecat?

2. For what reason does Hecat accuse the Witches of being "[s]aucy and overbold" (3.5.3)?

3. What do you notice about the meter and rhyme of Hecat's speech?

4. What does Hecat say she is going to do?

ACT 3, SCENE 6

1. Reread the entire scene and consider that by the end of Lennox and the Lord's conversation, Lennox has expressed his hope that "a swift blessing / May soon return to this our suffering country / Under a hand accursed" (3.6.47-9).

   a. How do Lennox and the Lord feel about Macbeth's reign?

   b. What are they hoping will happen?

   c. How is Macduff involved?

2. At first Lennox does not express directly his criticism of Macbeth's reign. Lennox's ambiguous report on the recent events in Scotland, which hints that he does not believe the official stories about Duncan's murder, is an example of equivocation. *(See "Larger Questions" number 12 on page 2 for an explanation of equivocation.)*

Reread 3.6.1-24. Make a list of phrases that suggest that Lennox equivocates and explain how each phrase works. I have done one as an example.

---

1. "the right valiant Banquo walked too late, / Whom, you may say, if 't please you, Fleance killed, / For Fleance fled" (3.6.5-7). Although Lennox reports that Fleance killed his father, Lennox does not specify that he himself believes that Fleance killed Banquo. Instead he says that the Lord "may" choose to believe this story if it "pleases" him. Lennox thus distances himself from the report by suggesting that believing the story would be for one's pleasure or convenience rather than because it is believable or true.

2.

3.

3. If you were directing the play, what would you instruct the actor playing the Lord to do during Lennox's opening speech (3.6.1-24)? What could the Lord do that would allow Lennox to become increasingly direct in his criticism of Macbeth's reign? Write a stage direction for the Lord to insert at a specific point in Lennox's speech. Indicate at what line you would insert the direction.

4. Using what you know about Macbeth's reign, explain why Lennox at first would equivocate rather than say directly how he feels about recent events in Scotland.

ACT 4, SCENE 1

1. What are the Witches putting into the cauldron?

2. Some of the ingredients come from human beings.

    a. List three such ingredients.

    b. What would a seventeenth-century English audience member notice that the human beings on this list have in common?

3. To what or whom does Witch 2 refer when she says, "Something wicked this way comes" (4.1.45)?

4. What does Macbeth call the Witches now? Quote the phrase.

5. When Macbeth asks the Witches what they are doing, they respond, "A deed without a name" (4.1.49). What would you name their deed?

6. Witch 1 interrupts Macbeth's question and tells him that he need not speak because the First Apparition "knows [his] thought" (4.1.69).

   a. What is the First Apparition?

   b. What does the First Apparition tell Macbeth?

   c. Judging from what the First Apparition tells Macbeth, what thought does the Apparition "know" Macbeth has?

7. Second Apparition.

   a. What is it?

   b. How does Macbeth respond when the Second Apparition says that "none of woman born / Shall harm Macbeth" (4.1.80-1)?

   c. If you were Macbeth, what might you wonder about the Second Apparition's prophecy having just heard the First Apparition's prophecy? Does Macbeth seem to compare the prophecies?

8. Third Apparition.

   a. What is it?

   b. What does the Third Apparition tell Macbeth?

   c. How does Macbeth respond to this news?

9. With what does Macbeth threaten the Witches if they "[d]eny" him an answer to his question about whether "Banquo's issue" will "reign in this kingdom" (4.1.102-5)?

10. What do the Witches show Macbeth?

11. How does Macbeth respond to this show?

12. Reread:

> Time, thou anticipatest my dread exploits.
> The flighty purpose never is o'ertook
> Unless the deed go with it. From this moment
> The very firstlings of my heart shall be
> The firstlings of my hand. And even now,
> To crown my thoughts with acts, be it thought and done. (4.1.144-9)

    a.   What does Macbeth pronounce should be the relationship between purpose and deed? Between heart and hand? Between thoughts and acts?

    b.   What had Macbeth said was "the pauser" (2.3.110)? _____

    c.   If Macbeth has decided not to pause before acting, what kinds of things might he do?

13. After hearing that Macduff has fled to England, what does Macbeth decide to do to Macduff's castle (4.1.150-3)?

ACT 4, SCENE 2

1. The scene begins in the middle of a conversation. Consider Lady Macduff's opening question, "What had he done, to make him fly the land" (4.2.1). What must Ross have just told Lady Macduff?

2. Lady Macduff describes how when the small, poor wren has young ones in her nest, she will fight against the owl—a much larger bird of prey (4.2.9-11). How does Lady Macduff use this fact about the wren to show that her husband "wants the natural touch" (4.2.9)? ("Wants" here means *lacks*.) What has Macduff done that Lady Macduff considers unnatural?

3. What might cause Ross to think that Macduff is "noble, wise, judicious" (4.2.16)?

4. What might Ross mean when he says that "cruel are the times when we are traitors / And do not know ourselves" (4.2.18-19).

    a. To what are they traitors? What about the time makes them so?

    b. How might their being traitors cause them not to "know" themselves?

5. Lady Macduff tells her son that a traitor is "one that swears and lies" (4.2.47). Given her definition, why would she tell her son that his father is a traitor? In other words, about what might Lady Macduff feel her husband has sworn and lied?

6. What point does the Son make about punishing traitors—"liars and swearers" (4.2.54-6)?

7. Lady Macduff refers to her assertion that she has "done no harm" as a "womanly defense" (4.2.76-77).

    a. What does she recognize about the "earthly world" that makes her know that even if one does no harm, one may still be punished or harmed (4.2.73)?

    b. What, then, is Lady Macduff implying it is to be "womanly"? Circle the best synonym:

       stupid   naïve   weak   fickle   hysterical

    c. Do you think Lady Macduff acts this way? Explain how or how not.

8. How does Macduff's son respond when the Murderer calls his father a "traitor" (4.2.80-1)?

9. With what evidence could you argue that Macduff is a traitor to Scotland?

10. With what evidence could you argue that Macduff is not a traitor to Scotland?

ACT 4, SCENE 3

1. The scene again begins in the middle of a conversation. Consider Malcolm's suggestion that they find "some desolate shade" and "Weep" (4.3.1-2). What news about Scotland would Macduff have been telling Malcolm?

2. Reread:

> Let us rather
> Hold fast the mortal sword, and like good men
> Bestride our downfallen birthdom. (4.3.2-4)

Make a quick sketch of Macduff's figure of speech. (*Bestride* means "to stand over (a fallen man) in order to defend him" (*OED* 2c); *birthdom* means "inheritance, birthright" (*OED* 1).)

3. Macduff's figure of speech contains a *metonymy* and a *metaphor*. (*See page 92 of appendix 2 for an explanation of* metonymy.)

For what is *birthdom* a metonymy? _____

For what is *bestride* the vehicle? _____

4. Malcolm suspects that even if Macduff is not "treacherous," Macduff might nonetheless consider it wise "To offer up a weak poor innocent lamb / T' appease an angry god" (4.3.16-18).

   a. Analyze his metaphor:

vehicle	:	tenor
weak poor innocent lamb	:	
angry god	:	

   b. What does Malcolm suspect Macduff might be there to do?

   c. What does Malcolm's metaphor suggest about how people may act under Macbeth's reign?

5. Malcolm reiterates his point that even if Macduff is good, he might do something bad under the command of a king: "A good and virtuous nature may recoil / In an imperial charge" (4.3.19-20). Do you agree with Malcolm's point about what may happen to a "good and virtuous nature"? Why or why not?

6. Reread:

That which you are my thoughts cannot transpose.
Angels are bright still, though the brightest fell.
Though all things foul would wear the brows of grace,
Yet grace must still look so. (4.3.21-4)

    a.   What does Malcolm mean when he says his thoughts "cannot transpose" what Macduff is?

    b.   What, according to Malcolm, is true about angels even though the "brightest" angel "fell"?

    c.   If something "foul" were to "wear the brows of grace," what would it look like?

    d.   What, according to Malcolm, is true about grace even if "all things foul would wear the brows of grace"?

    e.   EXTRA OPPORTUNITY. How do Malcolm's ideas about appearances compare to Duncan's assertion that "There is no art / To find the mind's construction in the face" (1.4.11-12)?

7. Malcolm asks Macduff, "Why in that rawness left you wife and child, / Those precious motives, those strong knots of love, / Without leave-taking?" (4.3.26-8). Why might Macduff's leaving his wife and child make Malcolm "doubt" Macduff (4.3.25)?

8. Notice the figures of speech Macduff and Malcolm use to describe their country. List two:

9. Reread what Malcolm says that he would do if he were king (4.3.50-99). List two of his claims.

10. What does Macduff say is a "tyranny" (4.3.66-7)?

11. Eventually Malcolm tells Macduff that he has been lying.

    a. What is Malcolm's motivation for telling these lies about himself?

    b. If you were Macduff and had traveled to England to bring Malcolm back to Scotland as king, how would you feel about Malcolm now?

12. Why might Macduff remain silent after Malcolm's speech that ends in the news that Malcolm has raised an army including "Old Siward with ten thousand warlike men" (4.3.134)?

13. To what "things" might Macduff refer when he says, "Such welcome and unwelcome things at once / 'Tis hard to reconcile" (4.3.138-9)? Give two possibilities:

14. What is the King of England reported to be able to do (4.3.140-59)? How does this report about the King of England compare to reports about Macbeth?

15. Speaking of the murder of Macduff's family, Malcolm tells Macduff, "Dispute it like a man" (4.3.220).

    a. What does Malcolm mean that Macduff should do?

    b. What does Malcolm imply it is to be "like a man"?

16. Macduff responds, "But I must also feel it as a man" (4.3.221).

    a. What does Macduff mean that he must do?

    b. What does Macduff imply it is to be "as a man"?

17. What "time" of Macduff's does Malcolm call "manly" (4.3.235)?

18. How do Malcolm's and Macduff's characterizations of being "like a man" or "manly" compare?

19. EXTRA OPPORTUNITY. Malcolm asserts that "Macbeth / Is ripe for shaking" (4.3.237-8).

    a. Analyze the metaphor:

       <u>vehicle</u>   :   <u>tenor</u>

    b. Which earlier metaphor about Macbeth does Malcolm's metaphor recall? To what effect?

ACT 5, SCENE 1

1. What does the Gentlewoman report to the Doctor about Lady Macbeth's condition?

2. Since when has Lady Macbeth been in this condition? (*Field* (5.1.3) here refers to the battlefield.)

3. What will the Gentlewoman not report (5.1.12)? Why might she refuse to do so?

4. What has Lady Macbeth commanded to have "by her continually" (5.1.19-20)?

5. What had Lady Macbeth wished for before Duncan's murder? (Look back at 1.5.)

6. "Yet here's a spot" (5.1.28). What is Lady Macbeth doing? Is she succeeding?

7. Reread Lady Macbeth's sleepwalking speeches and then answer the following:

    a. Does Lady Macbeth speak in verse or prose? Did she speak in verse or prose earlier? *(See pages 83-4 of appendix 1 for an explanation of* verse *and* prose.*)*

    b. What is she counting when she says, "One, two" (5.1.31)?

    c. Whom does she address and what might she mean when she says, "A soldier, and afeard? What need we fear who knows it, when none can call our power to account" (5.1.32-4)?

    d. Who is the "old man" (5.1.35)? What surprises Lady Macbeth about him? When would she have seen this?

    e. "Here's the smell of blood still. All the perfumes of Arabia will not sweeten this little hand. Oh, Oh, Oh!" (5.1.44-5). What had Lady Macbeth said on the night of the murder about cleaning up the blood? Quote the line:

f. EXTRA OPPORTUNITY. Choose something else Lady Macbeth says in the scene. Quote it and say whom she seems to address and when:

g. Look back at what Lady Macbeth tells her husband on the night they plan the murder. Where had Macbeth's letters about the Witches' prophecies "transported" her (1.5.54-6)?

h. Where do Lady Macbeth's sleepwalking experiences take her?

8. The Doctor says Lady Macbeth "[m]ore needs...the _____ than the physician" (5.1.66). Do you think he is correct?

ACT 5, SCENE 2

1. What do Menteith and Angus report about Malcolm, Siward, and Macduff?

2. What does Caithness report about Macbeth?

3. What does Angus say is motivating those whom Macbeth commands (5.2.19-20)?

4. EXTRA OPPORTUNITY. Analyze Caithness's metaphor: "He cannot buckle his distempered cause / Within the belt of rule" (5.2.15-16).

5. Angus remarks, "Now does he feel his title / Hang loose about him, like a giant's robe / Upon a dwarfish thief" (5.2.20-2).

    a. Analyze the simile:

vehicle	:	tenor
hang loose	:	
giant's robe	:	
dwarfish thief	:	

    b. What does this simile imply about titles? How does it add to the earlier metaphors for titles?

6. Where, according to Caithness, is "obedience . . . truly owed" (5.2.26)?

7. a. Analyze one of the following metaphors by charting its vehicles and tenors:

   "Meet we the med'cine of the sickly weal, / And with him pour we in our country's purge / Each drop of us" (5.2.27-9).

   or

   "Or so much as it needs, / To dew the sovereign flower and drown the weeds" (5.2.29-30).

   <u>vehicle</u>   :   <u>tenor</u>

   b. What idea of the "weal" does the metaphor reveal? ("Weal" here means *community* or *state*.)

8. EXTRA OPPORTUNITY. Analyze the second metaphor.

ACT 5, SCENE 3

1. Why does Macbeth ask, "What's the boy Malcolm? / Was he not born of woman" (5.3.3-4)?

2. What do you think of Macbeth's calling the fleeing thanes "false" (5.3.7)?

3. a. What does Macbeth say "should accompany old age" (5.3.24)?

   b. What does Macbeth's saying that he "must not look to have" such things reveal about his conscience (5.3.26)?

4. What does Macbeth ask the Doctor to do for his wife (5.3.39-44)? What metaphors does Macbeth use?

5. What does Macbeth ask the Doctor to do for his country (5.3.50-2)? What metaphor does Macbeth use?

ACT 5, SCENE 4

1. Why does Malcolm order every soldier to "hew him down a bough" (5.4.4)?

2. What do you now understand about the third apparition's prophecy?

ACT 5, SCENE 5

1. What does Macbeth explain with his statement that he has "supped full with horrors" (5.5.13)? Why "supped"? How has having supped full with horrors changed the way he reacts to horrors now?

2. Carefully reread Macbeth's speech that follows the announcement of his wife's death (5.5.17-28).

   a. "She should have died hereafter. / There would have been a time for such a word" (5.5.17-18). (*Hereafter* means "after this in time; at a future time; in time to come" (*OED* 2).)

   Such a word as what? _____

   Why might Macbeth think that "hereafter" there would have been time for this word?

   b. What is the effect of the repetition of the word "tomorrow"?

   c. What, according to Macbeth, does tomorrow do?

d. What do all our yesterdays do?

e. Analyze: "Out, out, brief candle" (5.5.23).

vehicle	:	tenor
candle	:	
brief	:	
out	:	

f. "Life's but a walking shadow, a poor player / That struts and frets his hour upon the stage / And then is heard no more" (5.5.24-6). With what two additional metaphors does Macbeth describe life?

g. Next Macbeth says life is a "tale" (5.5.26). What kind of tale? Quote the lines.

h. Consider Macbeth's description of the tale. How would it sound? Try to perform a bit of it!

3. What does Macbeth realize at the end of the scene when he says, "I . . . begin to doubt the equivocation of the fiend / That lies like truth" (5.5.42-4). Whom is he calling "fiend"? How does he explain equivocation?

4. Do you agree with Macbeth that he is the victim of equivocation? Why or why not?

ACT 5, SCENE 6

1. With what pronouns does Malcolm refer to himself (5.6.4-6)?   (Keep in mind that *upon's* is a contraction of *upon us.*)

2. What does this pronoun choice show about Malcolm?

ACT 5, SCENE 7

1. As what does Macbeth imagine himself (5.7.1-2)?

3. Macbeth tells the slain Young Siward, "Thou wast born of woman" (5.7.11). What does his statement reveal about his attitude toward the Witches and the prophecies?

4. What does Macduff say would cause his "wife and children's ghosts" to "haunt [him] still" (5.7.16)?

ACT 5, SCENE 8

1. Why does Macbeth say he has avoided Macduff (5.8.4-6)? What does this comment reveal about Macbeth?

2. What does Macduff inform Macbeth about his arrival into the world?

3. Who are "these juggling fiends" (5.8.19)? What does Macbeth say about them?

4. What does Macduff threaten to do to Macbeth? How would Macduff make Macbeth "the show and gaze o'th' time" (5.8.24)?

5. What does Siward say about his son's death (5.8.47-50)?

6. What earlier scene does Macduff's holding Macbeth's decapitated head echo?

7. What might Macduff mean when he announces that "The time is free" (5.8.55)? How had the time been confined?

8. a. What does Malcolm promise to his supporters?

   b. What earlier event in the play does this promise recall?

9. Reread Malcolm's final speech (5.9.60-75). What does his speech suggest about the kind of king he intends to be? Derive your answer from specific remarks.

10. Where will Malcolm be crowned? Who else was crowned there?

APPENDIX 1. LISTENING FOR METER—AN INTRODUCTION

Actors have long observed that Shakespeare's plays convey their meanings not only through the sense of his language but also through its sounds, including rhyme, alliteration (repeated consonant sounds), and assonance (repeated vowel sounds). Read aloud and consider how the sounds of a speech contribute to its meanings.

This section will help you get started listening for the rhythms of a Shakespeare play by introducing you to two meters you will encounter in *Macbeth*.

    & For most English literature, **METER** refers to a deliberate pattern of stressed and unstressed syllables.

    "Stressed" syllables are the syllables that get the most emphasis when a word or sentence is spoken aloud. (In the literature of some other languages, including Greek and Latin, meter is measured by the length rather than the stress of syllables.)

    Keep in mind that you can hear the meter in which a poet has composed a speech or poem even while you can hear how the poet has, at times, varied that meter.

    & In a Shakespeare play, speeches in **VERSE** are composed with a repeating pattern of stressed and unstressed syllables and are divided into deliberate lines. Verse is composed in meter.

    & In a Shakespeare play, speeches in **PROSE** are composed without a repeating pattern of stressed and unstressed syllables and are not divided into deliberate lines. Prose is not composed in meter.

An example of VERSE in *Macbeth*:

> *Macbeth*   Thy very stones prate of my whereabout,
>   And take the present horror from the time,
>   Which now suits with it. Whiles I threat, he lives:
>   Words to the heat of deeds too cold breath gives. (2.1.57-60)

    & *The last two lines of Macbeth's speech above, which have the same meter and end with a rhyme, are called a* ***COUPLET***.

- When you are reading verse, you will see that the word of each new line of a speech is capitalized whether or not it begins a new sentence.

- Whatever the size of a book's pages, printers retain the lines of a speech in verse. Thus, often you will see empty space between the end of a line and the right margin of your book's page. If a line of verse is longer than what fits on a particular page, then what remains of the verse line usually is indented and printed directly below.

- When you quote verse, you should retain the capital letters and indicate the line breaks with a forward slash, called a *virgule*. Example: Macbeth worries that the sound of his footsteps on the stones will "take the present horror from the time, / Which now suits with it" (2.1.57-8).

An example of PROSE in *Macbeth*:

> *Porter*   Here's a knocking indeed! If a man were porter of Hell
> gate, he should have old turning the key. *(Knocking within)*
> Knock, knock, knock! Who's there, i' the name of
> Beelzebub? (2.3.1-4)

- When you are reading prose, you will see that lines are printed until a word nearly reaches the right margin of the page. The word of a new line, which varies depending on the size of the book, is not capitalized unless it happens to begin a new sentence.

✍ A **TROCHEE** is a poetic foot of one stressed syllable (marked "/") followed by one unstressed syllable (marked "˘"). Examples of single words that are trochees are:

$$
\overset{/}{\text{thun}}\overset{˘}{\text{der}} \qquad \overset{/}{\text{bloo}}\overset{˘}{\text{dy}}
$$

✍ **TROCHAIC TETRAMETER** names the meter of a line with four ("tetra") trochees. Examples:

$$
\overset{/}{\text{Dou}}\overset{˘}{\text{ble,}} \overset{/}{\text{dou}}\overset{˘}{\text{ble}} \overset{/}{\text{toil}} \overset{˘}{\text{and}} \overset{/}{\text{trou}}\overset{˘}{\text{ble}}
$$
$$
\overset{/}{\text{Fire}} \overset{˘}{\text{burn}} \overset{/}{\text{and}} \overset{˘}{\text{caul}}\overset{/}{\text{dron}} \overset{˘}{\text{bub}}\overset{/}{\text{ble.}} \text{ (4.1.10-11)}
$$

$$
\overset{/}{\text{Fair}} \overset{˘}{\text{is}} \overset{/}{\text{foul}} \overset{˘}{\text{and}} \overset{/}{\text{foul}} \overset{˘}{\text{is}} \overset{/}{\text{fair.}} \text{ (1.1.10)}
$$

> ✍ *The meter of this last line, which lacks the unstressed syllable of the final trochee, is named* **CATALECTIC TROCHAIC TETRAMETER.**

✍ Marking the stressed and unstressed syllables of a line of verse in the manner above is called **SCANSION.** To **SCAN** a line of verse is to listen for and mark its stressed and unstressed syllables and to notice what kind and how many of the repeating foot make up the line. Scansion also includes noticing any variations in the meter of a line. *(See page 85 for examples of variations in meter.)*

🖎 An **IAMB** is a poetic foot of one unstressed followed by one stressed syllable. Examples of single words that are iambs are:

$$\smile \quad /$$
un·seamed

$$\smile \quad /$$
pro·nounce

🖎 **IAMBIC PENTAMETER** names the meter of a line of verse with five ("penta") iambs. An example:

$$\smile \ / \ \smile \ / \ \smile \ / \ \smile \ / \ \smile \ /$$
So fair and foul a day I have not seen. (1.3.39)

Many speeches of *Macbeth* are composed in iambic pentameter and some in trochaic tetrameter, but you will hear many variations in the meter. Below are two to listen for. Consider what a variation calls attention to and what it may add to a speech's meanings.

🖎 Some iambic lines replace one of the iambs with a trochee, a **TROCHEE SUBSTITUTION**. Here's an example of an iambic pentameter line that begins with a trochee substitution:

$$/ \ \smile \ \smile \ / \ \smile \ / \ \smile \ / \ \smile \ /$$
Stay, you imperfect speakers, tell me more. (1.3.71)

🖎 Some iambic lines end with an extra unstressed syllable. Such a line is said to have a **FEMININE ENDING**. An example:

$$\smile \ / \ \smile \ / \ \smile \ / \ \smile \ / \ \smile \ / \ \smile$$
A dagger of the mind, a false creation, (2.1.37)

A line of verse can be spoken by more than one character. Here is a single iambic pentameter line shared by Macbeth and Lady Macbeth:

Lady Macbeth
$$\smile \ / \ \smile \ /$$
Did you not speak?

Macbeth
$$\smile$$
When?

Lady Macbeth
$$/$$
Now.

Macbeth
$$\smile \ / \ \smile \ / \ \smile$$
As I descended? (2.2.16)

Note that this line, which ends with an extra unstressed syllable, also has a feminine ending.

APPENDIX 2. READING FIGURATIVE LANGUAGE—
AN INTRODUCTION TO METAPHOR, SIMILE, METONYMY, & SYNECDOCHE

Shakespeare's plays are famous for their figures of speech, which are rich in meaning and sometimes difficult to understand. What follows is an introduction to four key figures of speech—metaphor, simile, metonymy, and synecdoche—along with some techniques you can use as you work to understand them.

> ❧ A **METAPHOR** asserts that one thing is another thing and demands that we imagine how it can be so.

"A rose is a flower" is not a metaphor. A rose is **LITERALLY** a flower. Anyone could find this out by looking up "rose" in a dictionary.

"Love is a rose" is a metaphor because it demands that we imagine how love is like a rose. A metaphor can be understood as true only if taken **FIGURATIVELY**.

Our English word *metaphor* is borrowed from Greek. *"Meta"* means *trans-* or *across*, and *"phor"* means *port* or *carry*; thus, *metaphor* can be translated as *transport*. The metaphor above transports a *rose* from the world of gardening to explain something in the world of emotions, namely, *love*. Metaphors explain something in one world by transporting something from a distant world for comparison.

One way to analyze a metaphor is to sort its TENOR and VEHICLE, terms coined by I. A. Richards in his 1936 book *The Philosophy of Rhetoric*.

> ❧ The **TENOR** is the subject of the metaphor—what the speaker is talking about.

> ❧ The **VEHICLE** is what is transported for comparison to illuminate some quality of the tenor.

In the metaphor "love is a rose," *love* is the tenor and *rose* is the vehicle.

The combination of a metaphor's vehicle and tenor prompts you to recognize that you're hearing or reading a metaphor because the statement would be otherwise absurd or impossible. As Richards emphasizes, the interaction of the tenor and the vehicle produces the metaphor's meaning.

Take, for example, the opening of Shakespeare's Sonnet 68:

Thus is his cheek the map of days outworn,

When we read this line, we realize that a literal cheek cannot also be a literal map, and so we know that we're reading a metaphor. Here *cheek* is the tenor—what the speaker is talking about—and *map* is the vehicle—what the speaker has transported from the world of diagrams and paper and ink to describe "cheek" by comparison.

Sometimes it is helpful to sort the metaphor's vehicle and tenor in a chart:

vehicle	:	tenor
map	:	cheek

And sometimes it is helpful to sketch the metaphor, trying to show both its vehicle (map) and its tenor (cheek). Here is an example:

G. Minette

❧ A **SIMILE** asserts that one thing is "like" or "as" another thing and demands that we imagine how.

"Lucinda is like her grandmother" is not a simile. It is a **LITERAL** statement.

"Lucinda is like a hurricane" is a simile. It is a **FIGURATIVE** statement.

Of course we may have to figure out how Lucinda is like her grandmother, but comparing Lucinda and her grandmother—who both are human, female, and kin—doesn't demand that we use our imagination to find similarities in altogether different categories of things as we must if we are to understand how a human being is like a storm.

Like metaphors, similes work by comparison, but with the word *like* or *as*, similes indicate their comparisons more explicitly. Similes announce the relationship between the tenor and vehicle more formally. Lady Macbeth speaks a simile when she tells her husband:

Your face, my thane, is as a book[.] (1.5.60)

Here Lady Macbeth is talking about his *face* and has transported a *book* to describe it. You could chart the simile:

vehicle	:	tenor
book	:	face

The metaphor that opens Sonnet 68 articulates both tenor and vehicle—the cheek and the map—and makes clear their relationship: the cheek "is" the map. Sometimes, however, a metaphor does not name both tenor and vehicle. Or sometimes a metaphor does not state so clearly how the vehicle corresponds to the tenor. Such metaphors require more interpretation. Consider, for example, Macbeth's complaint:

> O, full of scorpions is my mind, dear wife! (3.2.36)

We know that Macbeth speaks a metaphor because a *mind* isn't a body part, like a *head*, that could be filled with scorpions. Plus, if some part of Macbeth were filled with literal scorpions, he probably would not be able to speak clearly!

Macbeth doesn't say explicitly what in his mind corresponds to the scorpions. So, we need to interpret. We can start by charting:

vehicle	:	tenor
scorpions	:	?

And we can then make a logical interpretation based on his statement's context. Sometimes that context suggests more than one interpretation. For instance, we could say:

vehicle	:	tenor
scorpions	:	guilty thoughts

Or we could say:

vehicle	:	tenor
scorpions	:	worried, terrified thoughts

Sometimes a statement or speech articulates more than one part of a metaphor's vehicle or tenor. Take, for example, Duncan's statement upon greeting Macbeth, which includes several vehicles associated with planting:

> *Duncan*   Welcome hither.
>   I have begun to plant thee, and will labor
>   To make thee full of growing. (1.4.27-9)

Here are four steps that can help lead to an accurate and productive analysis of such a metaphor. I have included sample analysis for each step.

STEP 1. IDENTIFY THE METAPHOR'S SPEAKER, AUDIENCE, & CONTEXT.

Jot down speaker and audience, and briefly review the immediate and relevant context of the speech.

Example:

Duncan to Macbeth. Duncan has just welcomed Macbeth and thanked him for his military service. Duncan has recently rewarded Macbeth by naming him the Thane of Cawdor.

STEP 2. IDENTIFY THE METAPHOR'S VEHICLES.

Underline all the elements of the metaphor's vehicle in the speech.

> *You can find a metaphor's vehicle by looking for the parts that would be absurd if taken literally with the tenor. Here you can recognize that "to plant" is part of the vehicle because it would be absurd to imagine that Duncan is telling Macbeth that he intends literally to insert him into a plot of earth and water him.*

Example:

Duncan   Welcome hither.
        I have begun <u>to plant</u> thee, and will <u>labor</u>
        To make thee <u>full of growing</u>.

STEP 3. SORT THE METAPHOR'S VEHICLE & TENOR.

A. Start by listing the elements of the vehicle and tenor the speaker states explicitly. Leave blank spaces for the corresponding parts of the vehicle and tenor implied.

Example:

vehicle	:	tenor
?_____	:	I (King Duncan)
to plant	:	?_____
?_____	:	thee (Macbeth)
(farm) labor (cultivate, etc.)	:	?_____
full of growing	:	?_____

90

B. Then, think about the analogies and fill in those blanks.

You might find it helpful to ask yourself questions like: "What has King Duncan begun to do to Macbeth that is like planting him?" Or: "What would Macbeth become that is like a plant's becoming "full of growing"?

You also might find it helpful to identify the worlds of the vehicle and the tenor. For instance, the vehicle here is from the world of farming or gardening and the tenor is from the world of politics and governance.

Remember that filling in the blanks requires interpretation and that there may be more than one way to interpret accurately.

Example:

vehicle (world of farming)	:	tenor (world of politics)
<u>gardener or farmer</u>	:	I (King Duncan)
to plant	:	<u>to place in leadership positions</u>
<u>seedling or seed</u>	:	thee (Macbeth)
(farm) labor (cultivate, etc.)	:	<u>political work (promote, favor, etc.)</u>
full of growing	:	<u>powerful</u>

STEP 4. ARTICULATE THE METAPHOR'S MEANINGS & IMPLICATIONS.

First, think carefully about the metaphor's specific vehicle. In the case of this metaphor, think about the qualities of planting and growing. Then, think about how the qualities of the vehicle are transported onto the metaphor's tenor.

Keep in mind that not all of the implications and meanings of a metaphor are necessarily intended by the character who speaks the metaphor. Even when a metaphor's implications may not be intended by a character, they nonetheless can acquire meaning in the play.

Example:

> If promoting Macbeth is like planting a seed or seedling, then King Duncan is like a farmer or gardener who will tend his plant. Since farmers and gardeners plant and cultivate seedlings in order to reap the benefits at harvest time when the plants have become "full of growing," the metaphor suggests that King Duncan can benefit from Macbeth's becoming powerful. If King Duncan is a farmer, the metaphor also suggests that although with his "labor" he can nurture the growth of Macbeth, he does not have total control. Other conditions, including good seed, the right amount of sun and water, and staying free from pests, are necessary for a plant's growth. Since what a farmer will harvest from a seed or seedling is never certain, Duncan's metaphor of planting Macbeth also introduces some uncertainty about what Duncan will "harvest" or gain from promoting Macbeth.

Whereas metaphor and simile work by comparison, metonymy and synecdoche work by association or scale.

☙ One thing standing for another associated thing is called **METONYMY**.

Macduff uses metonymy when he refers to Malcolm's pious mother, the queen, as having been "Oftener upon her knees than on her feet" (4.3.110). Being *upon one's knees* is associated with *prayer*, and the phrase "upon her knees" stands here for the act of praying.

Lady Macbeth uses metonymy when she says that she plans to remove "All that impedes" her husband "from the golden round" (1.5.26). *The golden round*—the crown—is associated with *kingship*, and the phrase *the golden round* stands here for the *kingship* more broadly.

☙ Part of a thing standing for the whole thing is called **SYNECDOCHE**.

Macbeth uses synecdoche when he orders the Servant who has brought bad news, "Take thy face hence" (5.3.19). A *face* is part of a *body*, and the word *face* stands here for *body*. Macbeth, thus, orders the Servant to leave.

The difference between *being associated with* and *being part of* can be very slim, so it can be difficult to decide whether to classify a figure of speech as metonymy or synecdoche. The difference between metonymy and metaphor, however, is larger and more significant. In order to understand a metaphor or simile we need to imagine how a tenor in one world compares to a vehicle from a distant world: we need to imagine how one thing *is* or *is like* another thing with which it ordinarily is not associated. Unlike metaphor and simile, metonymy and synecdoche are from the same world as the things they stand for.

APPENDIX 3. ON HOW AN EDITION OF *MACBETH* IS MADE

Shakespeare, who died in 1616, did not take part in the publication of his plays. The earliest extant text of *Macbeth* is found in a collection of Shakespeare's plays entitled *Mr. William Shakespeares Comedies, Histories, & Tragedies,* which was printed in London in 1623. Scholars now refer to this first edition of Shakespeare's collected plays as the *First Folio,* and all editions of *Macbeth* are based on it. You can compare your edition of *Macbeth* to the text included in the First Folio by finding a facsimile of it in your library or on the World Wide Web.

You will notice a number of differences between the First Folio and any modern edition of the play.

- **Editors standardize spelling and punctuation according to current practices.** So, for instance, the First Folio's lines,

> 2. When the Hurley-burley's done,
> When the Battaile's loſt, and wonne.

become in most modern editions,

> *Witch 2*   When the hurlyburly's done,
>   When the battle's lost and won.

- **Editors add stage directions not in the First Folio.** Often editors distinguish their own stage directions from those in the First Folio by enclosing them in parentheses or brackets. The First Folio, for instance, does not include a stage direction when, in act 2, scene 3, Lady Macbeth exclaims, "Helpe me hence, hoa." Most modern editions, however, include "*(fainting)*" or "*[fainting]*" before the line, "Help me hence, ho!" Editors base such stage directions on their reading of the play, so you should always test them by reading the lines closely and considering other possible stagings.

- **Editors add line numbers.** Although the First Folio divides the play into acts and scenes, it does not mark line numbers. Because some speeches in the play are in prose (not verse), a modern edition's line numbers vary depending on the size of the page. *(See pages 83-4 of appendix 1, "Listening for Meter," for explanations of* verse *and* prose.*)*

- **Editors include notes that explain selected words and phrases.** In some notes editors provide definitions for words whose meanings were different in Shakespeare's day or whose meanings might be unfamiliar to us now. For instance, editors often note that the word *behind* can mean "still to come." Editors do not list all possible definitions, but you can check the *Oxford English Dictionary* for a complete list of seventeenth-century meanings of any word. In other notes editors may offer more extensive explanations of the meaning of a phrase or a line. Read such notes critically: there may be additional ways to understand the phrase or line. *(See question 8c on page 6 for an exercise on reading an editor's note critically.)*

ACKNOWLEDGMENTS

Over the years I have had the pleasure of reading *Macbeth* with hundreds of students at Friends Seminary. Their enthusiastic interest in the play, their willingness to work to understand it, and their fresh interpretations have inspired me to develop and publish this guide. I am thankful to Lauren Simkin Berke for making the book's cover, not only because Lauren has done so with extraordinary insight and skill, but also because it feels particularly fitting to have the book covered in a Friends Seminary graduate's vision of the play. I am grateful to Robert Lauder, Principal of Friends Seminary, for his gracious support of this project and to my English Department colleagues for their enduring camaraderie and help.

I am grateful to Donna Anstey at Yale University Press for granting me permission to include, on page 93 of this guide, the scanned image of two lines of *Macbeth* from the 1954 Yale University Press facsimile edition of *Mr. William Shakespeares Comedies, Histories, & Tragedies*.

Special thanks goes to Heather Cross, who convinced me to make the guide available to the general public and who made key suggestions about its structure. I am grateful to Chris Doire, Cara Murray, Katherine Olson, and Sarah Spieldenner for their valuable comments on the guide's appendices and to Philip Kay for suggesting its preface. Patrick Morrissey's discerning reading of the manuscript and our many exchanges about meter, figurative language, and *Macbeth* greatly improved the guide's clarity and accuracy. Finally, I am grateful to Gordon Minette for his advice on matters large and small as I prepared the book for publication.